W9-BJN-155

BUGS

KINGFISHER
LONDON & NEW YORK

Copyright © Macmillan Publishers International Ltd 2017
Published in the United States by Kingfisher,
175 Fifth Ave., New York, NY 10010
Kingfisher is an imprint of Macmillan Children's Books, London
All rights reserved.

Distributed in the U.S. and Canada by Macmillan,
175 Fifth Ave., New York, NY 10010

Library of Congress Cataloging-in-Publication data has been applied for.

Series editor: Hayley Down
Designer: Jeni Child

ISBN (PB): 978-0-7534-7346-7
ISBN (HB): 978-0-7534-7345-0

Kingfisher books are available for special promotions
and premiums. For details contact: Special Markets
Department, Macmillan, 175 Fifth Ave.,
New York, NY 10010.

For more information, please visit
www.kingfisherbooks.com

Printed in China

9 8 7 6 5 4 3 2 1

1TR/0417/WKT/UG/128MA

Picture credits
The Publisher would like to thank the following for permission to reproduce their material.
Top = t; Bottom = b; Middle = m; Left = l; Right = r
Front cover: Shutterstock/Tomatito; Back cover: Shutterstock/yanikap; Cover flap: iStock/samuiboy; Page 1 iStock/step2626; 3 Alamy/Ken L Howard; 4–5 iStock/cicloco; 4t Shutterstock/Tharkul; 4b Alamy/Jens Brüggemann; 5t iStock/samuiboy; 5b iStock/engabito; 6 Shutterstock/moomsabuy; 7t Alamy/Martin Shields; 7m Shutterstock/Hawk777; 7b Alamy/Papilio; 8–9 Alamy/Frank Hecker; 10tl Shutterstock/irin-k; 10tr Shutterstock/IrinaK; 10ml Shutterstock/yanikap; 10mr Shutterstock/paulrommer; 10bl Shutterstock/Henrik Larsson; 10br Shutterstock/Linas T; 11tm Shutterstock/Marco Uliana; 11tr Shutterstock/Alexander Sviridov; 11tr (ants) Shutterstock/asharkyu; 11ml Shutterstock/thailoei92; 11br Shutterstock/Fablok; 12 (1) iStock/BarnabyChambers; 13tl (2) Shutterstock/7th Son Studio; 13tl (3) iStock/NNehring; 13ml (4) Shutterstock/Tharkful; 13bl (5) Alamy/Arco Images GmbH; 13bl (6) Alamy/blickwinkel; 13tr (7) iStock/vblinov; 13tr (8) iStock/Anest; 13mr (9) Shutterstock/Barnaby Chambers; 13br (10) Shutterstock/Maryna Pleshkun; 14–15 Alamy/Rafael Ben-Ari; 16–17t iStock/stanley45; 16bl iStock/TobyPhotos; 17bl Shutterstock/Hans Christiansson; 17br iStock/Musat; 18 Alamy/FLPA; 19t iStock/Joesboy; 19m iStock/gesnipes; 19b iStock/supershock; 20–21 Alamy/blickwinkel; 22 Alamy/Grant Heilman Photography; 23t Shutterstock/thatmacroguy; 23b iStock/freemixer; 24–25 Alamy/Jens Brüggemann; 26tl, bl (ants) iStock; 26tl, bl (ant nest) Shutterstock/Potapov Alexander; 26tr, br Shutterstock/Pan Xubin; 26m (ant nest) iStock; 26mr Shutterstock/Joy Tasa; 26mr (termite nest) Shutterstock/Mark52; 27tl, bl Shutterstock/HandmadePictures; 27ml Shutterstock/dwphotos; 27mr Shutterstock/SaraJo; 27br Shutterstock/Kletr; 28–29 Alamy/beerworawut; 29br Alamy/John Cancalosi; 30 iStock/SumikoPhoto; 31t Alamy/Mircea Costina; 31b Alamy/dpa picture alliance; 32–33 Alamy/ARCTIC IMAGES; 34 (1) Alamy/ephotocorp; 35tl (2) Shutterstock/Pavel Krasensky; 35tl (3) Alamy/Krystyna Szulecka; 35ml (4) Alamy/Jakub Gojda; 35bl (5) iStock/Henrik_L; 35bl (6) iStock/jeridu; 35tr (7) iStock/themorra; 35tr (8) iStock/wckiw; 35mr (9) Getty/Flick's Pix; 35br (10) Getty/Robert F. Sisson; 36–37 Alamy/age footstock; 38 Getty/ Kim Taylor; 39t iStock/mirceax; 39m iStock/Alex25; 39b Alamy/Johner Images; 40–41 iStock/WI6995; 41t iStock/samuiboy; 41m iStock/Bosca78; 42tr Getty/Gunter Fischer; 42br Alamy/blickwinkel; 43tl iStock/AlasdairJames; 43tr iStock/JanMiko; 43bl Shutterstock/Valerijs Vahrusevs; 43br Shutterstock/basel101658; 44 Getty/JodiJacobsen; 45t Alamy/Nature Picture Library; 45b Alamy/blickwinkel; 46–47 Getty/xbn83; 48tl AlamyAndySmyStock; 48bl iStock/IMNATURE; 48br iStock/Ian_Redding; 49tl iStock/OlijaSimovic; 49tr iStock/boryak; 49bl iStock/Yousef-Abuaisheh; 49br Alamy/Genevieve Vallee; 50–51 Shutterstock/Peter Schwarz; 52 iStock/engabito; 53t iStock/dagut; 53m iStock/CathyKeifer; 53b iStock/Gregory_DUBUS; 54 Alamy/imageBROKER; 55t Alamy/GFC Collection; 55b Alamy/Steve Taylor ARPS; 56–57 iStock/ithinksky; 58b iStock/ranplett; 59t iStock/imv; 59b iStock/RPFerreira; 60 iStock/Ian_Redding; 61 iStock peych_p; 62 Shutterstock/FloridaStock; 63 iStock/gui00878.

BUGS

BY BARBARA TAYLOR

KINGFISHER
NEW YORK

CONTENTS

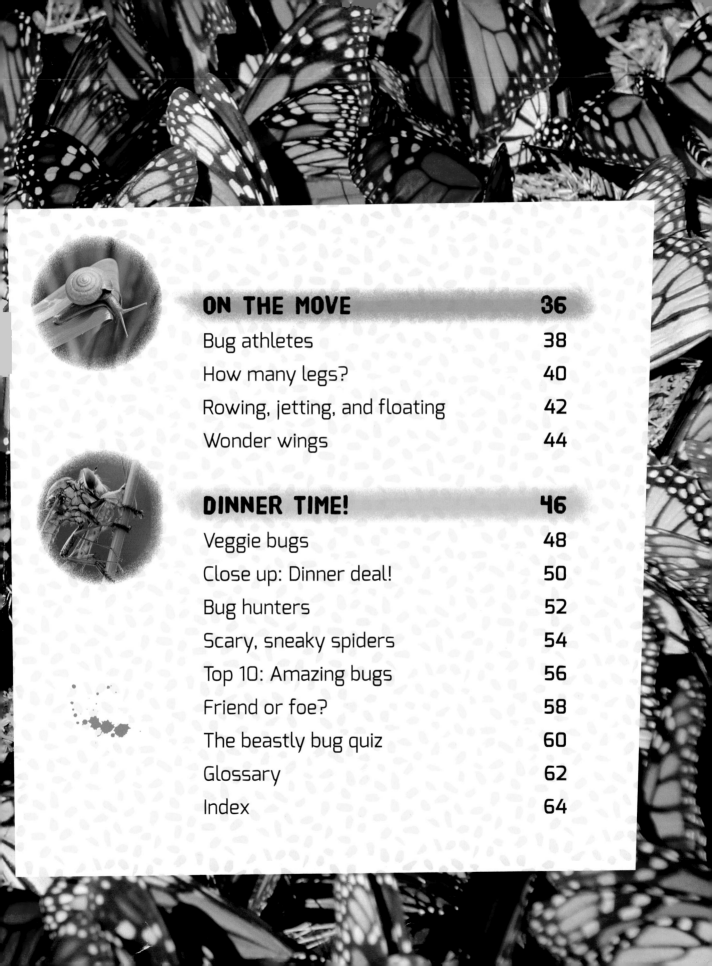

WHAT IS A BUG?

The bugs in this book have two main things in common: they are all small animals, and they do not have a hard skeleton inside their body. Their skeleton is usually on the outside (an exoskeleton). Bugs are also **cold-blooded**, which means their body is a similar temperature to their surroundings. Most live on land, although some, such as diving beetles, live in freshwater.

Bugs lived on Earth long before dinosaurs or people, and they make up more than 80 percent of all the different kinds of animals alive today—so bugs are the most successful creatures on the planet! Most bugs live on their own, but a few insects (such as ants) live and work together in large groups, which are like bug cities or towns.

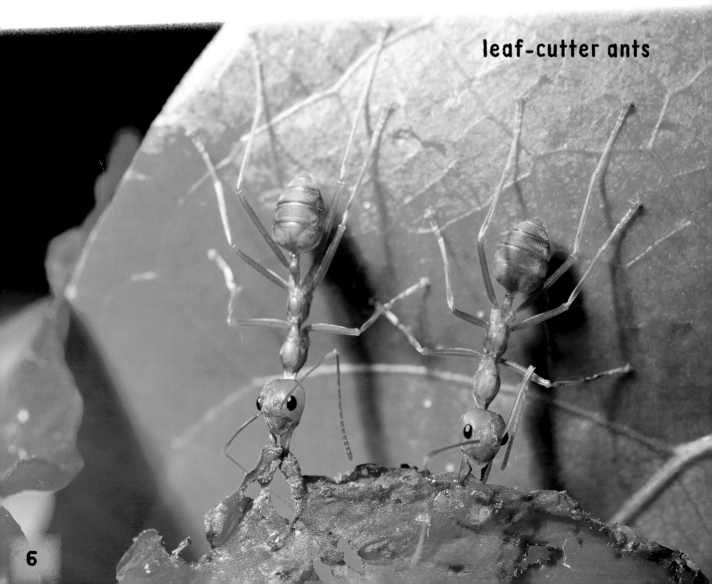

leaf-cutter ants

INSIDE YOU'LL FIND . . .

. . . giant beetles

Bugs are **SMALL** because their body doesn't work at a bigger size! A giant exoskeleton would crush a bug under its weight. The Hercules beetle is the world's longest beetle, and it's only as long as an adult hand!

. . . dragonflies

Insects were the first animals to fly, more than **350 MILLION** years ago. They are still the only group of invertebrates (animals without backbones) that has developed the power to fly.

. . . butterflies

Which bugs lead a **DOUBLE LIFE?** Some insects, such as butterflies, change shape completely as they develop. This means they can eat different food and live in different places, making them more successful than other bugs.

WHO'S WHO IN THE

Millions of small creeping, crawling, hopping, swimming, and flying bugs lurk on our planet. These minimonsters can be grouped according to features they have in common.

INSECTS

Insects have six legs and three body parts. A hard exoskeleton covers and protects an insect's body, like a suit of armor. Most insects have one or two pairs of wings. There are more than one million different kinds (**species**) of insects on our planet—and perhaps as many as five million species!

scarlet lily beetle

SPIDERS

Spiders have eight legs and two body parts, so they are not insects; they are arachnids! A spider never has wings, but it does have a hard exoskeleton and a shieldlike plate (carapace) to protect the front part of its body. There are more than 40,000 species of spiders, but only about 30 kinds of spiders are dangerous to people.

jumping spider

WORLD OF BUGS?

CENTIPEDES

Centipedes have a long, flat body with an exoskeleton divided into **segments**. Each segment except the last one has one pair of legs. Centipedes have venomous claws to kill their prey. They are related to millipedes, which are not venomous and usually have two pairs of legs per segment. There are more than 10,000 species of millipedes and more than 3,000 species of centipedes in the world.

WORMS

Worms have a long, thin, squishy body with no legs at all. They do not have an external skeleton, and they keep their shape using fluids inside their body. Many worms are **parasites** that live on or in other animals and take food from them. There are more than one million species of worms, including about 3,000 species of earthworm, which have a segmented body.

slimy earthworms

centipede

TOP 10 SURVIVAL CHAMPS

Which bugs are the best survival champions of all?

Ultimate survivor

Cockroaches have lived on Earth for about 340 million years. They have hardly changed over time because they are so well **adapted** for survival. They live just about everywhere and eat almost anything. They can live for up to a month without food—and can even survive a nuclear explosion!

2 Bloodsucker

The Draculas of the bug world, bed bugs bite sleeping humans at night and suck up tasty, human blood!

7 Dragon caterpillar

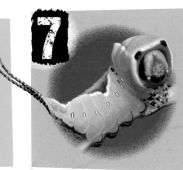

Puss moth caterpillars act like tiny dragons. They puff up their body, whip their tail, and spray poison—but they don't breathe fire!

3 Magic trick

When is a stick not a stick? When it's a stick insect that looks so much like a stick, it can disappear . . . as if by magic.

8 Can't hurt me . . .

Did you know that snails and slugs can glide over a sharp knife without hurting themselves? Their slime protects their soft body.

4 Spider silk

Silk made by spiders, such as this funnel web spider, is stretchier than rubber and stickier than tape!

9 What a stink!

If they are attacked, stinkbugs squeeze out a horrible liquid that smells so bad it sends **predators** running for cover!

5 Snorkel bug

A water scorpion has a built-in "snorkel" at the end of its body. When it needs to take a breath of air, it pushes its "snorkel" above the water's surface.

10 Wormtastic

Earthworms cannot see or hear, but they can breathe through their skin and live for four to eight years.

6 Armor-plated

A pill millipede rolls into a ball if it is attacked. The thick "armor" on its back creates a hard shell, which protects its soft belly.

Which survival champion is your number one?

MONARCHS LOVE MILKWEED!

Monarch butterflies lay their eggs on milkweed plants. Once hatched, the caterpillar eats the milkweed—in fact, it is the only plant that monarch caterpillars eat! Monarchs are also called milkweed butterflies because they need the plant to survive.

More about monarchs:

Adult wingspan: 3.5–4.1 in. (9–10.5 cm)
Average life span: 6–8 months
Food: milkweed
Other names: milkweed, common tiger, wanderer, black-veined brown

1 2 3

LIFE CYCLES

Most bugs hatch from eggs. Some baby bugs look like tiny adults when they hatch, but many look completely different!

CHANGING SHAPE

Many insects, such as beetles, butterflies, moths, flies, bees, and ants, hatch out of their eggs as soft, wormlike grubs, called larvae. A larva changes into a pupa before turning into an adult. This four-stage life cycle is called metamorphosis, meaning "change of body shape."

caterpillar

1 EGG: The larva hatches out of an egg and eats the shell as its first meal.

2 LARVA: The larva spends most of its time eating and growing, shedding its exoskeleton each time it grows bigger.

3 PUPA: When it is fully grown, the larva turns into a resting stage, called a pupa. Inside the pupa, the body of the larva is broken down and rebuilt into an adult with wings.

4 ADULT: The pupa's skin splits and the adult pulls itself free. Its wings are very soft. After its wings dry and harden, the adult flies to find a mate and begin the life cycle again!

LOOK-ALIKES

Bugs such as snails, worms, spiders, stick insects, and centipedes look like tiny versions of their parents when they hatch out of their egg. They may chew their way out of the egg or have spines on their body to help them break free. The baby bugs feed and grow, shedding their exoskeleton each time and growing a bigger one. This is because the exoskeleton will not stretch.

snails

GROWING WINGS

Bugs such as cicadas (si-cay-dahs), earwigs, grasshoppers, cockroaches, and termites have no wings when they hatch, only tiny **wing buds**. These wingless babies are called nymphs. As the nymphs grow, their wings develop and they have to shed, or molt, their exoskeleton several times. The tight "overcoat" splits and the bug wriggles out of its too-small exoskeleton. Eventually, it becomes an adult with wings.

cicada nymph

LIFE IN TWO WORLDS

Dragonflies have a three-stage life cycle: egg, nymph, and adult. Females lay their eggs inside the stems of water plants, and the nymphs that hatch out of the eggs live underwater. When a nymph is ready to turn into a dragonfly, it climbs out of the water, molts into an adult with wings, and flies away.

DANGER!

After molting, a bug's outer skin is soft. This makes it vulnerable to attack until its skin hardens.

BABY BUGS

Most female bugs do not take care of their eggs and babies. They usually lay their eggs in safe places where there is plenty of food for the young bugs. For instance, dung beetles lay their eggs in balls of dung, while acorn weevils lay their eggs inside acorns so the young are surrounded by food when they hatch.

Some female bugs provide a protective screen for their eggs. Pond snails lay their eggs in a mass of jelly, worm and spider eggs develop inside a **cocoon**, and some mantids produce a frothy substance that hardens around their eggs. Spittlebug nymphs produce their own mass of white bubbles, which stops the nymphs from drying out as well as hiding them from predators.

baby
trap-door
spiders

giant water bug

A few bugs, such as this male **GIANT WATER BUG**, carry their eggs or young around with them. The bug cannot move easily with his heavy load of eggs. He also cannot feed for several weeks until the eggs hatch.

green lynx spider

Did you know that female spiders are caring parents? The **GREEN LYNX SPIDER** uses silk-producing tubes (spinnerets) at the back of her body to attach her egg case to leaves with silk threads, like the ropes on a tent.

earwig with eggs

A female **EARWIG** guards her eggs until they hatch. She keeps the eggs clean and safe from predators. When the nymphs hatch, she coughs up food for them to eat!

Male **FIREFLIES** glow to attract females. Different species have their own pattern of flashing lights.

PERFECT PARTNERS

From perfumes and presents to music and dance, bugs use all kinds of signals to find the perfect partner.

Male **CICADAS** use drumlike structures on their **abdomen** to produce a **courtship** song made up of a stream of clicking sounds.

DEATHWATCH BEETLES knock their head on wood at night to attract a mate. These sounds were once thought to be very unlucky when heard by sick people.

The male **BUZZING SPIDER** beats his abdomen against a leaf to attract a mate.

Male **MOTHS** have huge, branched **antennae** (feelers) to pick up the scent of female moths. Each species of moth has a different scent.

Male **MOLE CRICKETS** sit at the mouth of their **burrow** and make purring sounds to attract females.

Male **JUMPING SPIDERS** try to impress females by doing a special dance—twirling, waltzing, and waving their legs and mouthparts in the air.

Male **HANGING FLIES** give their mate a gift of prey wrapped in silk so they are not eaten themselves during courtship and **mating**.

ROMAN SNAILS stab each other with "love darts" during courtship.

Male **STAG BEETLES** use their antlerlike jaws to wrestle with rivals for a mate. They may fight to the death!

LIVING
TOGETHER

BURIED CITY

ant nest

Ant nests are built
either underground
or in mounds of soil,
twigs, and leaves
above the surface. Inside are tunnels and
chambers, with separate rooms for food
and waste, nurseries for the young ants, and
a large chamber for the queen ant. Wood
ants live in huge nests, with up to 500,000
ants living together.

TREETOP NEST

termite nest

Most termites nest underground,
but some build nests high in the
trees instead. The nests of tree
termites are usually made from tiny
fibers of wood mixed with termite
saliva (spit). This mixture dries
as hard as rock, helping protect the
tiny fragile termites inside
from predators and bad weather.

CITIES

Some insects, called **social insects**, live in large groups, called colonies. Colonies may contain hundreds, thousands, or even millions of bugs!

BUSY BEEHIVE

beehive

Bumblebees live in small **colonies** of between 50 and 600 individual bees. They nest in rocky holes, grassy **hollows**, or old nests made originally by mice or birds. The queen bumblebee makes small wax cups (cells) and lays her eggs inside. Worker bumblebees hatch out of the eggs and help to care for the developing young. They even fan their wings to keep the young bees cool on hot days!

PAPER PALACE

hornet nest

Hornets build the largest nests of all the social wasps. Their round nest can be as large as a basketball and contain up to 25,000 hornets. The hornets make their nests from "wasp paper," which they produce by chewing plant fibers and mixing them with saliva to form a papery paste. Inside the nest are many stories made up of six-sided cells in which the young hornets grow.

TINY TEEMING ANTS

Your questions about life in an ant nest answered!

weaver ants

Which ants are good at sewing?

Weaver ants join leaves together to make their nests in rainforest trees. The larvae produce sticky silk threads. Some adults squeeze the larvae to release the threads, while others stitch the leaves together. The larvae are like living glue sticks!

Why do some ant armies live inside thorns?

The bull's horn acacia tree has armies of ants living inside its hollow thorns. The tree provides the ants with food and a safe home. In return, the ants patrol the tree like an army, driving off any insects that try to eat the tree. They also kill any plants that grow too close to the tree by blocking out sunlight and using up valuable **minerals** in the soil.

Which ants look like jars of honey?

Honeypot ants live in dry places or deserts in Africa, Australia, Central America, and North America. To help the colony survive during dry seasons, some of the largest worker ants store honey inside their swollen stomach. These ants hang from the roof of the nest without moving—like living jars of honey!

HONEYBEE HIVE

Wild honeybees nest in tree holes, but people also keep bees in specially built wooden boxes, called hives. The bees produce wax inside their body and use this to build rows of six-sided cells. Inside the cells are eggs, developing bees, and stores of **pollen** and honey. The cells fit closely together to form flat sheets called combs, or honeycombs.

Honeybees live in larger colonies than any other bee—one hive may contain up to 70,000 honeybees. Most of these are female worker bees, who collect food and guard the hive and the developing bees. One big queen bee lays all of the colony's eggs. At certain times of the year, male bees, called drones, hatch out of the eggs. They mate with new queen bees to start new colonies. After mating, the drones die.

How do honeybees collect POLLEN? The worker bees collect flower pollen in hairy "baskets" on their back legs. They can carry almost half their body weight in pollen.

BEASTLY FACT

honeybee

drinking nectar

Honeybees make **HONEY** by drinking flower **nectar** and converting it into honey in a special stomach. The honeybees use the honey as a food supply to help them survive cold winter weather.

BEASTLY FACT

growing up

BEASTLY FACT

Inside wax cells, honeybee **EGGS** hatch into soft larvae. Worker bees feed flower pollen to the larvae. The workers seal the fully grown larvae in their cells while they turn into pupae and then adult bees.

queen bee

The huge **QUEEN HONEYBEE** (centre) is larger than the workers. She is an egg-laying machine, producing up to 2,000 eggs in one day! She can live for up to five years, but worker bees live for only six weeks.

BEASTLY FACT

CLOSE UP

TERMITE TOWERS

Termite colonies are huge! They contain hundreds of thousands, or even millions, of termites. Even though a termite is only the size of a matchstick, millions of them build giant chimneys to let hot air escape from their underground nest. For their size, termites build the largest structures of all creatures!

More about termites:

Size: up to 1 in. (25 mm) long
Average lifespan: 1–2 years
Food: dead plants
Weird fact: Most termites are blind!

SOCIAL INSECTS

Which are the most extraordinary social insects?

1 Queen termite

A queen termite can lay up to 36,000 eggs a day. Her body is swollen into a gigantic sausage-shaped bag that is so big the queen termite cannot move!

2

Harvester ant

Harvester ants make bread! They grind up seeds to make the bread, which they store and use as a source of food all year.

3

Compass termite

Australian compass termites build nests with flat sides. The nest's shape keeps the bugs cool in the midday heat!

4

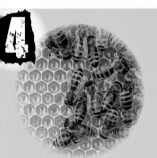

Honeybee

Jars of honeybee honey have been found in the tombs of the ancient Egyptians. Hundreds of Egyptian remedies were based on honey.

5

Carpenter ant

Carpenter ants build their nests in rotten wood and produce sawdust, just like human carpenters. They can damage furniture by burrowing inside it.

6

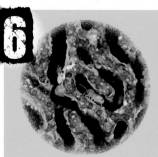

Termite

Termites make mounds out of a mixture of soil, wood, poop, and saliva, which sets into a rock-hard material.

7

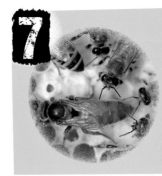

Queen honeybee

A queen honeybee makes a scent (smell) to tell her workers she's alive—and prevent any of them from developing into new queens.

8

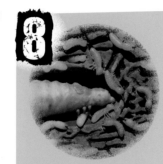

Soldier termite

Soldier termites defend themselves with huge jaws. These work like sharp scissors, slicing their enemies into pieces.

9

Leafcutter ant

Leafcutter ants are very strong for their size and some of them can lift up to 50 times their own body weight.

10

Fig wasp

Fig wasps lay eggs inside figs. The eggs develop, and adult females emerge and fly away. Wingless male wasps die inside the figs.

Which social insect is your number one?

ON THE
MOVE

BUG ATHLETES

Some bugs are much better athletes than people! Those with long legs are sprinting champions, while others would easily win medals at the Olympics for the long jump! Water bugs are excellent swimmers, and some can even walk on water! Bugs with wings take to the air, some of them flying marathon distances across whole **continents**.

Bugs need to be good at sprinting, jumping, swimming, and flying so they can escape from danger and predators. Bugs travel to find food, new places to live, and safe resting spots. Bugs also travel in order to find a mate and survive from generation to generation.

BEASTLY FACT

JUMPING SPIDERS are champions of the long jump. Some can leap more than 40 times their body length! Before it jumps, the spider fixes itself with a safety line of silk in case it falls.

jumping spider

tiger
beetle

Champion **SPRINTERS** in the bug world are tiger beetles! Their long legs take big strides to cover up to 2 ft. (60 cm) per second—that's about 125 body lengths! A human can run only four body lengths per second.

Grasshoppers can **JUMP** 20 times their own body length. That's like a person jumping the length of a basketball court! Grasshoppers have springy knees and very powerful muscles in their back legs. Leaping is faster than walking, helping grasshoppers escape danger!

grasshopper

Flies, such as houseflies and bluebottles, can walk **UPSIDE DOWN** across a ceiling with no problem at all. They have hooks and sticky pads on their feet to help them grip smooth surfaces easily.

bluebottle

HOW MANY LEGS?

How do bugs move with lots of legs or no legs at all? Your questions answered.

How do bugs move without any legs?

Snails move on top of a big piece of muscle called a "foot." The muscle ripples from front to back in waves, moving the snail along. A snail produces a trail of thick slime to help it glide along more easily.

Why don't millipedes trip over their legs?

Millipedes have 45 to 300 pairs of legs, but they move slowly. A millipede's legs move in waves, with groups of legs swinging forward while other groups of legs swing backward. This helps stop the millipede from tripping up!

Why do some caterpillars loop the loop?

Inchworms, also called looper caterpillars, have no legs in the middle of their body. The caterpillar brings its back legs next to its front legs, making the middle of the body form a loop, then stretches its front legs forward to take a step. This is not a quick way of moving!

Why do some spiders turn cartwheels?

The golden wheel spider is a remarkable gymnast. When threatened, it throws itself sideways, pulls in its legs, and rolls into a tight ball. Then it can turn cartwheels down sand dunes to escape quickly from danger.

ROWING, JETTING

Hairy legs, water skis, and jet engines are just three of the adaptations that help water bugs move.

common backswimmer

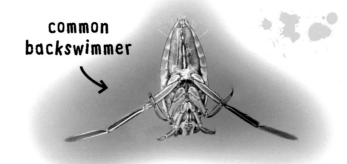

WATER SKIER

To escape predators, the water lily beetle skis across the water's surface so fast it seems to disappear! Claws on its feet have tiny hairs to repel water and stop the beetle's feet sinking through the surface. The beetle flaps its strong wings fast and bounces on the water's surface as if it is using a pogo stick! This beetle water skis at speeds of about 1.6 ft. (0.5 m) per second!

waterlily beetle

ROWBOATS

Water boatmen row through the water with legs that work like oars. These bugs have extralong back legs, fringed with long hairs. The hairs increase the **surface area** of the legs, which brush water aside as they beat up and down to push the bug through the water. The hairs also trap air bubbles so the bug can take its own air supply underwater.

water boatman

AND FLOATING

common pond skater

dragonfly
nymph

JET ENGINES

Did you know that dragonfly larvae have built-in jet engines? If a dragonfly larva is disturbed or attacked, it can suddenly squeeze water out of the back of its body. This gives it a short burst of jet propulsion, somewhat like a jet engine moving a plane through the air. The water squirting backward pushes the larva forward, helping it escape danger.

dragonfly larva

WATER WALKERS

Some bugs can walk on water without the help of magic! Water has a thin, springy "skin," and these bugs are small and light enough not to break through it. A water spider's long, thin legs spread out its weight over a big area. The water's surface bends under the spider's feet like a trampoline, but it does not break.

water spider

A butterfly's wings are covered in tiny **SCALES**, as seen up close in this picture. They absorb warmth from the sun and insulate (keep warm) the butterfly's wings.

WONDER WINGS

Flying is a fast way to travel but uses a lot of energy. Night fliers warm up their muscles before taking off.

LOCUSTS have reserves of fat that last for up to 20 hours of flight.

* In the same time that you can **BLINK**, some flies can beat their wings a thousand times!

* The best fliers in the world are **FLIES** and **DRAGONFLIES**, which twist and turn through the air like tiny helicopters.

* Some **HAWK MOTHS** can fly at speeds of up to 30 mph (50 km/h)—that's as fast as a car! Their narrow wings are shaped like those of a jet airplane, helping these moths zoom along.

* **LARGER BUGS** beat their wings more slowly. Honeybees beat their wings up to 200 beats per second, whereas a large swallowtail butterfly beats its wings only five times per second!

ladybug

* The flying wings of **LADYBUGS** are protected by a pair of tough wing cases. When they fly, ladybugs hold their wing cases up and flap their flying wings.

VEGGIE

Bugs may eat any part of a plant, from its roots to its flowers. Some even grow their own food, like human farmers!

DRINKING STRAWS

Strawlike mouthparts are useful for sucking up liquid food. Adult butterflies and moths have a long, tubelike tongue, called a proboscis, for sucking up sugary flower nectar. This high-energy food helps power their wings. Other bugs, such as aphids and cicadas, pierce plants with a sharp, pointed mouthpart and suck up the plant sap through a long tube.

butterfly

CHEWING JAWS

Grasshoppers and caterpillars have powerful cutting and chewing jaws that bite through tough plant leaves. A grasshopper's jaws work like a pair of pliers to cut through the leaves. Grasshoppers are messy eaters, often tearing the leaves as they feed. Leaves don't contain many nutrients, so bugs have to eat a lot of leaves to take in enough energy to live and grow.

grasshopper

BUGS

NAIL-FILE TONGUE

Snails and slugs don't have mouthparts or teeth to cut and chop up their food. Instead, they use a rasping tongue, called a radula, to scrape off pieces of plants or scoop plant food into their mouth. The ribbonlike radula is covered with thousands of sharp, backward-facing points, called denticles, which are arranged in interlocking rows.

snail

BUG FARMERS

Leaf-cutter ants cut pieces of leaves from plants. These pieces are many times the size of the tiny ant and are carried back to an underground nest. (This is like a person carrying a small van on their back!) Inside the nest, the ants use the leaves to make a mushy compost for a fungus garden that feeds millions of ants. The ants eat the fungus they grow because they cannot digest the actual leaves.

leaf-cutter ants

CLOSE UP

DINNER DEAL!

When it is a caterpillar, the chalkhill blue butterfly produces a sweet, sugary food that yellow meadow ants eat! The ants take a caterpillar into their underground nest, where they can eat the food it produces. In return for the food, the ants keep the caterpillar safe until it turns into an adult. Animals that work together like this have a symbiotic relationship.

More about chalkhills:

Wingspan: 1.3–1.6 in. (33–40 mm)
Food: the horseshoe vetch plant
Weird fact: Chalkhill caterpillars eat
only the horseshoe vetch plant. This
means they always live on the chalky
hills where this plant grows.

BUG HUNTERS

Fierce and feisty bug hunters catch and kill other animals. Some stalk and chase their **prey**, like miniature lions. Others spring a nasty surprise by jumping out from a hiding place or setting a trap to catch their supper. Bugs that **ambush** their prey like this are often well **camouflaged** so that they can get really close to their victims before they attack.

Bugs may crush or crunch up their prey with powerful jaws or inject **venom** that **paralyzes** or kills their prey. Robber flies use their hairy legs to trap prey as they fly. Then they inject venom to turn the insides of their victim into a mushy soup and soak up the meal through spongelike mouthparts.

robber fly

SCORPIONS use their claws to capture their prey and stop it from escaping, somewhat like cats. A scorpion's giant pincers hold its prey in a very tight grip. Then the scorpion uses its strong jaws to pull its meal to pieces and crush it to a soft pulp.

scorpion

A **MANTID** keeps very still while it waits for an insect to come within reach. Then the mantid shoots out its spiked front legs at lightning speed to grab the meal. It starts eating while the prey is still alive!

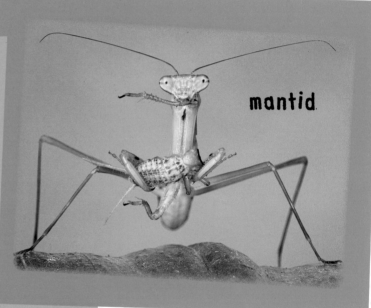

mantid

ant lion and prey

ANT LIONS dig pits in sand and soft soil and then wriggle inside, leaving just their jaws showing. Bugs slip into the pit, falling straight into the waiting jaws of the ant lion.

Hundreds of **DOME-WEAVER SPIDERS** build webs together to form a "spider city." They may hunt over this web city in packs.

SCARY, SNEAKY SPIDERS

About half of all the spiders in the world trap their prey in sticky webs.

CRAB SPIDERS match the colors and patterns of the flowers on which they hide. They are able to kill bugs much bigger than themselves, such as bees.

SPITTING SPIDERS squirt sticky **poison** over their victims, pinning them to the ground so they can't escape.

The **BOLAS SPIDER** catches moths on a silken fishing line. It whirls this line around and around, trapping the moths on a sticky drop at the end of the line.

One teaspoon of **SPIDER SILK** would be enough to make a million webs.

A **TRAP-DOOR SPIDER** lurks inside an underground burrow. It waits patiently for small bugs to trip over thin lines of silk that it has cunningly placed around the entrance. Then it leaps out to grab a meal.

LYNX SPIDERS and **WOLF SPIDERS** are athletic hunters that chase after their prey. They may even eat others of their own kind, making them **cannibals**!

Some spiders are very venomous indeed. The **BRAZILIAN WANDERING SPIDER** has the largest venom glands of any spider. These glands hold enough venom to kill 225 mice!

Large **TROPICAL SPIDERS** build huge orb webs up to 6.5 ft. (2 m) across. These webs are strong enough to catch small birds.

55

TOP 10

AMAZING BUGS

Come face to face with our top 10 most unusual bugs!

1 Peacock spider

Just like the bird it is named after, the male peacock spider has a colorful trick for mating time! He lifts the brightly patterned flap of his abdomen, raises his legs, and dances to attract a female.

2. Orchid mantid

This bug's colorful body is shaped like orchid flower petals, which helps to attract insect prey into its waiting jaws.

3. Giraffe weevil

Just like giraffes, these bugs have an extralong neck! Males have a longer one, which they use to fight each other for a mate!

4. Flower crab spider

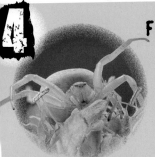

These spiders lurk on flowers waiting for a meal. They spring a surprise ambush when prey comes close!

5. Scorpions

Scorpions glow under UV light! They may sense UV light reflected by the Moon, and this may help them to find prey or shelter at night.

6. Long-horned orb-weaver spider

This bug has huge horns. Why? It's a mystery! They might scare off predators.

7. Treehopper nymph

This baby treehopper's weird hairdo is actually a waxy substance that scares away predators.

8. Hummingbird hawk moth

Just like a hummingbird, this moth hovers in front of flowers to suck up nectar with its tube-like tongue.

9. Panda ant

This bug wears a double disguise—it's not a panda, or an ant! It is actually a type of wasp with a very strong sting.

10. Ermine moth

Just like a hummingbird, this moth hovers in front of flowers to suck up sweet nectar with its tube-like tongue.

Which bug do you think is the most amazing?

FRIEND OR FOE?

Which bugs help us or harm us? Your questions answered.

aphids

Why do bugs damage our crops and possessions?

People think of many bugs, such as aphids, as pests because they feed on food crops. However, meat-eating bugs, such as ladybugs, help us get rid of bug pests. We need to find a balance between our own needs and the needs of the bugs that share our world.

Why are bugs good for the planet?

Without bugs that feed on animal dung, dead bodies, and rotting plants, our world would be buried under mountains of waste. Dung flies recycle animal poop, burying beetles feed on dead animal bodies, and dead leaves provide food for bugs such as worms, woodlice, and millipedes!

Which bugs make us sick?

Female mosquitoes have to suck human blood so that their eggs will mature and develop. Some kinds of mosquitoes also spread diseases, such as malaria and yellow fever, when they feed. Female blackflies suck human blood and may pass on parasitic worms that can cause blindness. Other bloodsucking bugs include bedbugs and head lice.

How do bugs help flowers?

Many flowers rely on bugs, such as ladybugs, to carry their pollen from flower to flower. The bugs visit the flowers to feed on sugary nectar and accidentally pick up the yellow pollen dust. Bugs that spread pollen between plants are very important to farmers growing fruit trees.

THE BEASTLY BUG quiz

Are you an expert on all things relating to bugs? Test your knowledge by completing this quiz! When you've answered all of the questions, turn to page 63 to check your score.

 1 What is the name for a skeleton on the outside of an animal's body?
a) Axoskeleton
b) Exoskeleton
c) Outerskeleton

 2 Which kind of bug could survive a nuclear explosion?
a) Butterfly
b) Bumblebee
c) Cockroach

 3 How many kinds (species) of insects are there?
a) More than 100,000
b) More than 500,000
c) More than one million

 4 How many kinds of spiders are dangerous to people?
a) 30
b) 300
c) 3,000

 5 Which of these bugs is related to millipedes?
a) Ant
b) Centipede
c) Mantid

 6 What does a pill millipede do when it is attacked?
a) Curls into a ball
b) Lies on its back
c) Runs away

 7 Which plant do monarch caterpillars eat?
a) Daffodil
b) Milkweed
c) Rose

 8 What is the name for a bug's feelers?
a) Antennae
b) Aerials
c) Andes

 9 Which insect looks like a honeypot?
a) Honeypot ant
b) Honeypot bee
c) Honeypot wasp

For its size, which insect builds the biggest structure of all creatures?
a) Cicada
b) Grasshopper
c) Termite

 Which kind of bug does not have a queen?
a) Honeybee
b) Tarantula
c) Termite

 What is a snail's muscly body called?
a) An arm
b) A foot
c) A leg

 Which bug can run at 2 ft. (60 cm) per second?
a) Bluebottle
b) Jumping spider
c) Tiger beetle

 How many eggs can a queen termite lay in one day?
a) 36
b) 360
c) 36,000

 Which insect makes bread?
a) Baker ant
b) Harvester ant
c) Kneading ant

 Where do carpenter ants build their nests?
a) In rotting wood
b) In the soil
c) Underneath rocks

 What is a proboscis?
a) A curly antenna
b) A pointed tail
c) A tubelike tongue

 Which animal glows under UV light?
a) Cockroach
b) Dung beetle
c) Scorpion

 What do honeybees use to make honey?
a) Flower leaves
b) Flower nectar
c) Flower petals

 How many webs would one teaspoon of spider silk make?
a) 100
b) 100,000
c) One million

GLOSSARY

abdomen
The rear part of a bug's body. It contains the digestive system.

adapted
A bug with body parts that make it suited to its way of life.

ambush
To hide and wait, then make a surprise attack on prey.

antennae
Long bodyparts on a bug's head that are used to sense the world around it, by feeling or sensing smell.

burrow
A hole or tunnel dug by an animal.

camouflage
The colors and patterns on a bug's body that help it blend in with its surroundings.

cannibal
An animal that eats others of its own kind.

chamber
A room or compartment.

cocoon
A silk bag or shelter made by some caterpillars (especially moth caterpillars), inside which they grow into adults. A spider's silky egg case is also called a cocoon.

cold-blooded
Describes any animal whose body temperature varies with the temperature of its surroundings. Cold-blooded animals cannot control their own body temperature.

colony
A number of related living things that live closely together in large groups. Social insects, such as ants, termites, and some kinds of bees and wasps, live in colonies.

continent
One of the seven big land masses of the world: Africa, Europe, North America, South America, Asia, Oceania, and Antarctica.

courtship
Behavior, such as dancing and singing, that forms a bond between a male and a female bug before they mate.

fiber
Strong, thin thread made by plants as part of their structure.

hollow
An empty space that curves inward.

mating
When a male and a female animal come together to produce young.

mineral
A natural solid that forms crystals. Minerals do not come from animals or plants, but living things need them to stay alive.

nectar
A sugary liquid produced by a flower to attract insects, such as bees and wasps.

paralyze
To make an animal powerless and unable to move, even though it is still alive.

parasite
An animal that lives on, or inside, another animal (its host), but does not usually kill its host.

poison
A substance produced by many insects that is harmful to touch.

pollen
A dustlike yellow powder that is produced by flowers, and is needed to make seeds.

predator
An animal that hunts and eats other animals for food.

prey
An animal that is killed and eaten by another animal.

segments
Regular divisions in the body or legs of an animal, that look like a series of rings.

social insects
Insects, such as ants, that live with others of their own kind in a large group, sharing tasks such as gathering food,

species
A group of living things that share similar characteristics and can breed together to produce young.

surface area
The amount of area covered by the outer part or the uppermost layer of something.

venom
A poisonous liquid produced by many insect predators and almost all spiders. Venom is injected into prey or enemies to hurt or kill them.

wing bud
A part of an insect nymph's body that will grow into wings as it develops into an adult.

QUIZ ANSWERS: 1 = b, 2 = c, 3 = c, 4 = a, 5 = b, 6 = a, 7 = b, 8 = a, 9 = a, 10 = c, 11 = b, 12 = b, 13 = c, 14 = c, 15 = b, 16 = a, 17 = c, 18 = c, 19 = b, 20 = c.

INDEX

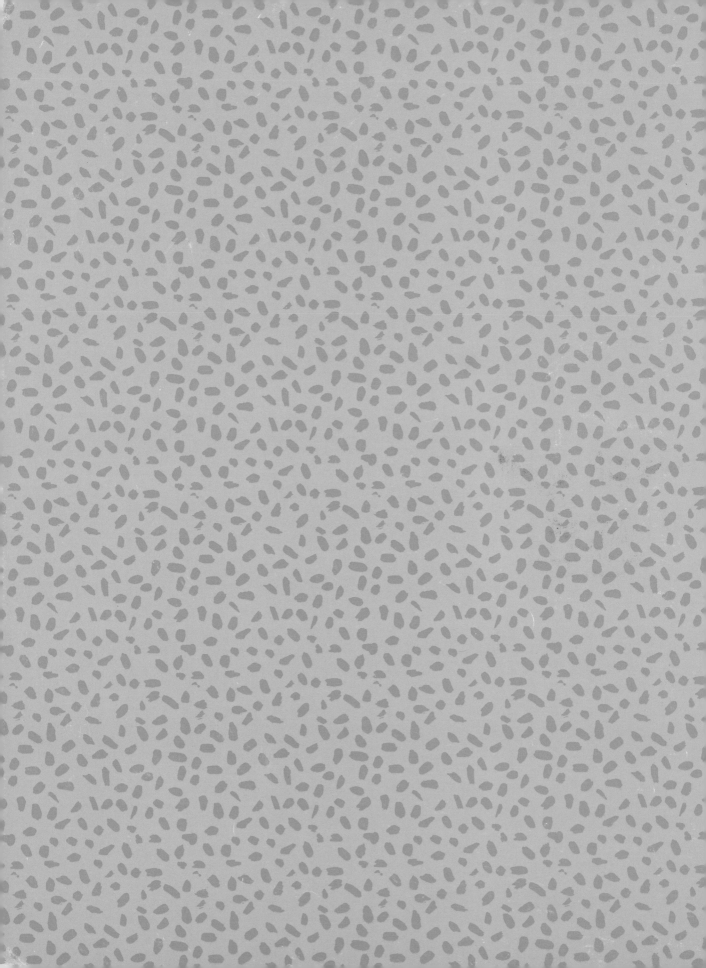